light in the Desert

Photographs from the Monastery of Christ in the Desert

BY TONY O'BRIEN

WITH AN ESSAY BY CHRISTOPHER MERRILL
FOREWORD BY MARY ANNE REDDING

Museum of New Mexico Press   Santa Fe

Foreword

IN 1995, PHOTOGRAPHER TONY O'BRIEN began a year of living and photographing in the secluded Benedictine abbey of Christ in the Desert, near Abiquiu, New Mexico, as a practicing member of this small contemplative community situated in the Rio Chama valley about seventy-five miles north of Santa Fe. The monastery is surrounded by miles of government-protected wilderness, thus assuring and promoting solitude and quiet for the cenobitic life. During his stay, O'Brien was given free access to photograph the rituals and daily activities, both contemplative and secular, at the monastery. The resulting images not only portray a continuing relationship between the photographer and the community of monks at Christ in the Desert but constitute an important body of creative work.

Spiritual inspiration motivates first individuals and then a community to gather to select or consecrate a site for ritual. In 1964, Father Aelred Wall and two other Benedictine monks discovered the isolated canyon while searching for a secluded place to found a new monastery. Father Aelred was seeking a contemplative life that would closely emulate the Rule of Saint Benedict in his cave in Subiaco, Italy. Over time these chosen places are invested with greater meaning as rituals are imprinted on the land. The chosen place becomes the site of prayer. According to theologian, writer, social activist, and Trappist monk Thomas Merton, who also photographed at Christ in the Desert when he visited for a week in 1968, "A monastery is not a place where a few men retire to deepen their own experience of the meaning of life; it is also a center where others can come to readjust their perspectives.... It remains a sanctuary where both monks and retreatants, Christians, believers in other faiths and those with no religious belief at all may experience something of that 'peace which the world cannot give.'" This is what O'Brien sought when he returned from his time as a POW in Afghanistan, retreating to the high desert to readjust his perspective about the time he spent as a prisoner and also about the life he was leading back at home in New Mexico.

O'Brien was drawn to the harsh beauty of the Chama canyon, a place he still regularly visits by himself and with his family—all of whom are intimately connected to the monastery and the monks who live there. Occasionally, O'Brien will take a lucky few to introduce them to this place he is so warmly connected with. No one leaves without feeling deeply moved by the place, its spirit, the brothers one meets, and the stories O'Brien narrates in his rich melodious voice, punctuated every so often by rolling his eyes toward heaven and belting out "for the love of God" or "God help us." The day Daniel Kosharek, Tom Leech, Nick Chiarella, and I made the journey from Santa Fe was on the feast of St. John the Baptist, who is the patron saint of the monastery. It was on this feast day that Father Aelred arrived in New Mexico forty-six years ago. We can only presume that his journey, like ours, was on a beautiful late-spring day, when even the light promises benediction. The drive was pleasant. It isn't always so easy to make the last thirteen miles of the drive into the canyon over dirt roads in the winter, after the spring thaws, or during monsoon season. The difficulties of the road, as some of O'Brien's photographs attest, become a metaphor for the difficulty of the journey to the monastery for those seeking solitude and welcome by the brothers. Many of us harbor a romantic idea that the monastic life is a life of ease. It isn't. It is a choice that, like marriage or being an artist, requires the deepest commitment. After three years of preparation and prayer, one of the brothers was making his final vows on the day we visited, and the community was invited to share in the celebration. The man's elderly parents were in the small chapel holding on to each other, obviously very moved and proud and brimming with happiness. I felt like a spy in the house of God, deeply stirred but a bit uncomfortable until Abbot Philip Lawrence welcomed us with a smile. Everyone was included in the impish light dancing in the abbot's bright eyes.

I think for O'Brien it was only by living at the monastery for a year, truly being part of the community, that he was able to understand the process of being that the monks manifest and to relax into the rhythms of the community in order to enjoy the process of photographing without the background noise of the world and its demands. During the time O'Brien lived at the monastery, the camera became his instrument of contemplation. In his images the deep quiet black is broken by rays of hot, white light in which details are not obscured but glow with a deeper detail that he is somehow able to capture on film. His gift becomes our gift. I have heard that a life well lived was to figure out one's gift and then to give it back. Seeing O'Brien's photographs, I am now beginning to understand what this means.

Many of O'Brien's images from this book will be featured in an exhibition at the New Mexico History Museum in Santa Fe beginning in October 2011 until early January 2013. *The Contemplative Landscape* showcases black-and-white photographs of sacred locations and landscapes in New Mexico which pay tribute to an ascendant ritual authority or serve as places of individual contemplation. Many of the images will explore the idea of sacred community performing in landscape. Through the generosity of John Scanlan and the Scanlan Family Foundation, the Photo Archives at the Palace of the Governors/New Mexico History Museum acquired twenty of O'Brien's images from the Monastery of Christ in the Desert portfolio, which was the seed that generated the exhibition. *The Contemplative Landscape* will also include historical photographs from the collections in the museum's photo archives as well as images selected from contemporary photographers who have explored New Mexico's contemplative landscapes: the land, art, architecture, and people who build and populate the sacred in its many manifestations.

MARY ANNE REDDING
Curator of Photography
Palace of the Governors/New Mexico History Museum

Introduction

CHRISTOPHER MERRILL

The bell rings in the dark, calling the monks to vigils, the night prayer that marks the beginning of each day at the Monastery of Christ in the Desert, in northern New Mexico. For Christian faith is itself a vigil, a watch to keep, and the monks chanting the Psalms in the adobe chapel, in the Liturgy of the Hours, add their voices to a tradition dating back to the origins of the faith, when Christ's followers gathered in Jerusalem to pray for His return. Now in the high desert the monks prepare for the Day of Judgment, sacrificing earthly desires for the promise of heaven: spiritual athletes training for eternity. And as light fills the red-rock canyon they begin the Divine Office of Lauds, the dawn prayer: *Praise the Lord*, they sing. *Praise God in His sanctuary*.

In this sanctuary by the Chama River, seventy-five miles north of Santa Fe, monks of the Benedictine order live in true austerity, following the Primitive Observance, which in its simplicity recalls the life of Saint Benedict, the father of Western monasticism. Tradition holds that Benedict was born in 480, in Umbria, in the chaos and carnage of the disintegrating Roman Empire; that as a young man he renounced the world and went off to live in a cave in Subiaco, not far from Rome, where he devoted himself to God, withstanding all manner of temptation; that despite his love of solitude he began to attract disciples, who persuaded him to become their abbot, and so it was that he established the first of more than a dozen monastic settlements. Eventually he compiled a rule for monastic life, based in part on the teachings of Saint Basil the Great, the fourth-century divine from Cappadocia, in which he defined "the tools of the spiritual craft"—tools that for nearly 1,500 years have helped men and women to forge closer relationships to God.

Monks, according to Thomas Moore, find in *The Rule* "the outlines of a life dedicated to community and contemplation"—a life discovered daily in the Monastery of Christ in the Desert. Through prayer and work, obedience and humility, the monks cultivate the virtues necessary for the journey to God—faith, hope, and charity. Chanting Psalms is their main responsibility (*Opus Dei*, the work of God), and seven times a day they proceed into the church to join their voices in praise and thanksgiving, working through all hundred and fifty Psalms not once but twice each week, reciting the verses attributed to King David and his court poets with a quality of attention designed to shape them in the image of God: a lifelong vocation.

The story begins in 1964, when Father Aelred Wall, Benedictine from the Mount Saviour Monastery in Elmira, New York, secured his abbot's blessing to purchase a farmhouse and 115 acres in the Chama valley. There on the floodplain, under towering cliffs and the harsh desert sunlight, Father Aelred set to work with brothers from Mount Saviour and volunteers from the surrounding communities to build a monastery. It was a return to the origins: just as Christ spent forty days and nights in the desert, preparing for His ministry, refusing the devil's temptations to commit the sins of gluttony, avarice, and pride, so thousands of men and women in the fourth century fled cities in Egypt to test themselves in the desert, translating their efforts to practice the Word of God into a body of wisdom, a collection of sayings and stories known as *The Evergetinos* (a new translation is available from the Center for Traditionalist Orthodox Studies): inspiration for monks like Father Aelred and his companions, who sought to worship in the remotest circumstances, surrounded by the Carson and Santa Fe national forests, at the end of a thirteen-mile-long dirt road that was not maintained very well.

They did not have an easy time of it. (Mari Grana provides a charming account of the monastery's first five decades in *Brothers of the Desert,* 2006.) Here is a story of false starts, seemingly insurmountable difficulties, and personality differences that periodically threatened to tear the community apart: the complications of a life that from the outside looks simpler than it is. For the founding of a monastery is a distinctly human enterprise, and since it is in the service of the divine, the contrast between its spiritual aspirations and the conditions on the ground are inevitably heightened. With varying degrees of hope, the monks planted a vegetable garden and orchard, built several two-room adobe structures in which to live, and raised a chapel, designed by the architect George Nakashima, in the shape of a Greek cross, with four wings extending from the clerestory and a bell tower that Thomas Merton, who visited the monastery twice in the months before his untimely death, likened to "a watchman looking for something or someone of whom it does not speak"—an effect that contemporary visitors may experience at the sight of the cliff rising behind the altar, filling the spacious windows.

After lauds comes Mass, the Eucharist, in which the monks, reenacting the Last Supper, receive the bread of heaven, the sacrament of His real presence, His continuing ministry in the world here below; and after breakfast they return to their cells to relax, pray, or read Scripture in a prayerful manner. *Lectio divina*, holy reading, is an essential element of monastic life (along with liturgical prayer and manual labor), in which a biblical passage may become the occasion for deeper communion with God. The monk meditates on the Word until there is no one and nothing else in his mind—a kind of attention that runs counter to the currents of modernity. Novices and postulants reinforce their reading with classes in Scripture, church and monastic history, and *The Rule* until the bell rings for the office of terce, when Christ was condemned to death. This is the first of three Little Hours (the others are sext and none), after which it is time to work, for as Saint Benedict reminds us, "Idleness is the enemy of the soul."

Thus the monks spend their mornings gardening, book- and beekeeping, preparing meals, fashioning handicrafts for sale in the gift shop and in a retail store in Santa Fe, cleaning the guesthouse, and performing maintenance. A monastery should be self-sufficient, and if the Monastery of Christ in the Desert has not always lived up to this ideal, the mere fact of its survival into the new millennium suggests that it will endure. Indeed its foundation has become secure enough for it to take on two dependent monasteries in Mexico—La Soledad, near San Miguel de Allende, and St. Mary and All the Saints in Xalapa—and one in Chicago.

Hospitality is offered to all who are willing to adhere to the schedule of work and prayer, and guests come from around the world to experience some of the riches of monastic life—the occasional pleasure of reflection, the continual possibility of grace. On retreat, guests listen less to the chatter of social life than to the chanting of the Psalms, heeding the Lord's promise: "What the eye hath not seen nor the ear heard, God has prepared for those who love him." Saint Benedict considered a monastery to be an ideal place to learn to love God, and the Monastery of Christ in the Desert is a splendid workshop filled with "the tools of the spiritual craft."

An early visitor to the monastery was Thomas Merton, the Trappist monk whose writings on the contemplative life have inspired generations of spiritual seekers. After his first pilgrimage into the canyon, in May 1968, he decided that these Benedictines had chosen the perfect place to recover the desert spirit of Christian monasticism:

The Monastery of Christ in the Desert is only in its beginnings: it is a small seed, seeking to fix its roots firmly in the rock and sand of the canyon, like the hardy piñon pines around it. It does not have the monastic ambitions of the big institutions which have become famous, for one reason or other, in various parts of the country. It seeks only to keep alive the complete simplicity of authentic Benedictine monasticism in its most primitive form: a communal life of prayer, study, work and praise in the silence of the desert where the Word of God has always been best heard and most faithfully understood.

For Merton the desert was the place to see "the true proportion of all things." And in September 1968, at the start of his ill-fated journey to the Far East, he came to see the Monastery of Christ in the Desert as "a place where all may experience the peace which the world cannot give." He was living in a time of great change and violence, little different from our own time or indeed that of Saint Benedict, and his was a voice of conscience—for social justice and civil rights, against the nuclear arms race and the Vietnam War. It occurred to him that a fruitful dialogue between different religious leaders and political figures might be fostered with the establishment of an East-West center, perhaps in the Chama canyon. This was one of the matters that he intended to discuss with Buddhist friends during his journey to India and Thailand, and it is tempting to imagine where such conversations might have led, had his life not been cut short. (He was accidentally electrocuted in his room, while in Bangkok for an interfaith conference.) What wisdom might have issued from a forum led by a thinker who understood the role that monasticism could play in creating a more just world? "The monk is always and essentially a man of prayer and penance," Merton wrote in *The Silent Life*. "His horizons are always and essentially those of the desert." And it is in the desert that fresh insights arise, some of which may save us.

For example, this story from the Desert Fathers, which Merton included in *The Wisdom of the Desert* (1960):

> A brother in Scete happened to commit a fault, and the elders assembled, and sent for
> Abbot Moses to join them. He, however, did not want to come. The priest sent him a
> message, saying: Come, the community of the brethren is waiting for you. So he arose
> and started off. And taking with him a very old basket full of holes, he filled it with
> sand, and carried it behind him. The elders came out to meet him, and said: What is
> this, Father? The elder replied: My sins are running out behind me, and I do not see
> them, and today I came to judge the sins of another! They, hearing this, said nothing
> to the brother, but pardoned him.

In such pardon lies the hope of the world. And this was what the war photographer Tony O'Brien discovered in the course of documenting a year of life in the Monastery of Christ in the Desert. Monasticism inculcates a prayerful attention to every moment, every task and gesture, and these photographs capture moments in the lives of men who day by day build the ark of the church, in a silence brimming with meaning. After sext, for instance, when the monks gather in the refectory for the main meal of the day, they eat in silence, listening to a reading from the Bible or a commentary on the text. And after none, the last of the Little Hours, the monks have an hour of *lectio divina*, followed by silent prayer in the chapel—the prelude to vespers.

O'Brien's riveting photographs reveal the silence at the heart of monasticism—the sacred aspect of every object and encounter, prayer and procession, shadow and light. The clock of ordinariness becomes the only measurement of time for this battle-hardened journalist; after the ravages of war in Afghanistan, he discovers in the silence of the monastery a resonating silence in his soul, translating his experience into works of sacred art, finding in casual details—a desk, a guest sweeping, fluttering sheets of music—the spiritual side of life here below. His photographs do not freeze time so much as suggest the timelessness of faith: the eternal present.

Thus a monk examining vestments at his sewing machine stitches seams to hold together the entire world, the fabric of faith that prompted a woman to touch the hem of Jesus's garment, with the hope of being healed. Daily we rend the fabric of faith, of life, and in the monk's service to God we learn how to make of our continual unraveling a robe in which to present ourselves to Him. This is the divine service that O'Brien renders in his photographs, which possess an air of finality, the silence of dusk, *the peace that passeth understanding* celebrated in the last office of the day, compline, the night prayer: "I will lie down in peace," the monks chant, "and sleep comes at once, for you alone, Lord, make me dwell in safety." And then silence.

These photographs make that silence sing.

light in the Desert

From My Journel: 1995

TONY O'BRIEN

MAYBE IT HAPPENED WHEN I FIRST LAID EYES ON NADR ALI, when I entered the prison cell having just been captured by the Afghan secret police. Or maybe it was when I tried to thank God, or the gods, and the only people present were the old man and the blind man, keepers of the neighborhood mosque in Kabul, as war raged about us. I had just learned Nadr Ali was alive, just released from prison, and that he remembered me. Or was it when our first child, Kiera Rose, was born, that I really believed that there was a God?

Maybe it was all of those things and more that brought me here to this small Benedictine monastery in northern New Mexico along the Chama River. This place of quiet solitude that is tucked between the canyon walls etched with the colors of the history of creation. As Thomas Merton, the Trappist monk and Catholic author, wrote, it's "a place of communal life of prayer, study, work, and praise in the silence of the desert, where the Word of God has always been heard."

Oh God, come to my assistance;
Oh Lord, make haste to help me.
—THE DESERT FATHERS

I entered as a photographer. My idea, to do an in-depth photography project on contemplative life, spending two weeks a month at Christ in the Desert. I soon found that this was more than a professional quest; it was a spiritual and personal one as well.

On the drive in I realize that I'm thinking about Afghanistan and Nadr Ali. We had shared a cell and a lifetime together. I had been imprisoned in Afghanistan while working on a story for *Life* magazine. It's this country: high desert, rock cliffs, and open space. I sometimes forget how hard and unforgiving it is. With beauty comes a hard reality.

I have beaten the snowstorm, but as I sit in my cell after the light meal, gray snow clouds slowly creep in, and before one notices, the clouds are low and gray, blocking out the sun, blue sky, and canyon walls. My cell has a desk with a kerosene lamp that sits in front of a small window looking out onto the path and mud road leading to the chapel and the canyon walls across the Chama River. I stoke the fire in my wood-burning stove. Once again I have found myself a resident of a cell.

I am always anxious when I come, yet upon seeing and greeting the monks, all doubts vanish. My days will begin at 4 a.m. with vigils, and then back to my cell for a shower, shave, and lection. Lauds at dawn in the chapel, celebrating the triumph of life over death, light over darkness, followed by fifteen minutes of quiet time, then breakfast in silence.

Prayer defines the contemplative monastic life. The day is divided into Divine Offices: specified times of prayer. The year too is divided into a sacred cycle. I will follow the ancient *Rule* of Benedict throughout my stay, following the daily cycle of prayer starting with vigils. As Abbot Philip says, "It is a time of longing, longing for the light. We sing the Psalms, praying the light will come." Following is lauds, prime, terce, sext, none, vespers, and finally compline at 8 p.m. Mass is celebrated daily. Each is a coming together of the community to pray—a constant reminder of one's purpose. I'm reminded of watching Nadr Ali pray five times a day, eventually joining him in prayer, following the Muslim cycle. He praying to his God and me to mine.

I spoke with Abbot Philip, all is a go. I am now an observer, the first step to "monkdom," no longer a guest.

I am living the life of a monk. I woke up apprehensive about my new status, Brother Tony. It was a beautiful walk to chapel for vigils. The stars were out, and the earth and winter foliage covered with snow. I took my place in choir and realize Xavier the hermit is on my right. It has begun.

Tonight I went to compline—the time to thank the Lord and bid the world good night. It is reassuring. We ask forgiveness and prayers, and ask the Lord and angels to protect us against the demons of the night. It is as if, like a child, we ask our father and mother to come to us and protect us from the unknown. They wrap their arms around us as we collapse in their protection.

It is a clear night, the sky awash with stars. Having forgotten my flashlight, I grope my way back to my cell without falling off the path. First rule of Benedict, take the damn flashlight.

I think of Petra, wife and friend, and Kiera. I love them so very much. They are my foundation and always are with me. How fortunate and blessed I am.

In prison we had discussed freedom, family, and faith. "Are you married?" he had asked. "Do you have children?" We had been talking of family. He was convinced that God and family were the most important things of life. Nadr Ali was perplexed, I was not married. "You must get married, Tony. Have a family." He was married with two children, and his father had died while he was in prison.

In the spring of 1993, in an adobe church in Santa Fe, I was married. The monks from Christ in the Desert sang Gregorian chants. Brother Bernard performed the ceremony, calling on Nadr Ali as a witness in absentia. The monks danced at the reception, and the abbot allowed each to kiss the bride—but only once.

On this visit, I arrived with a lot of baggage, none of it good.

As I told Bernie, I have felt like Job these last three days. Blessed Bernie, my Nadr Ali of the monastery, he was my savior yesterday. I left home truly angry. The time in chapel was devastating. I was within myself, fighting my own demons. I could not escape. There were moments when I thought the marriage was over.

I recall a day in our barren prison cell. I had fallen into the abyss, slumped against the wall, my hopes shattered. A shaven head appeared at the foot of the bed, and with arm raised Nadr Ali said, "Don't worry, Tony, God will take care of us."

I believe more and more this story is about myself. It's my search and quest for my God. In being honest with myself, I am being responsible to the Creator and mankind. We should take care of our lives spiritually and physically. My friend Jim Wolf said, "You are not at the monastery for pictures. You are there to find yourself. The spiritual journey, that is the main purpose."

I wept today. It is something I have not done since Kabul and the mosque after having discovered Nadr Ali was alive. I had gone to try and find someone to thank, only to find the old man and the blind man. It happened at Mass, when we exchanged greetings of peace. It is something I have needed to do for a long time.

Holy Week is getting into full swing, and Philip is the celebrant for the Mass. During the homily he spoke again about forgiveness and betrayal. It takes me back to memories of my capture and the two who betrayed me in the "safe house" in Kabul, after our meal together. Judas and Peter were the topics of the Gospel.

I am forty-nine years old today. It is the Sabbath, and I am in a monastery. Think about that. I spoke with one of the monks at recreation last night, telling him about how my adjustment from guest to monk has been a bit daunting. He said, "It's interesting to think about. My happiest moments were as a guest." We both laughed. It is not necessarily the Zen experience one imagines. Six a.m. and I am off to lauds. Ah, the monastic life, and I am married and have a child. It has been an intriguing life.

Philip discusses from *The Rule* of Benedict, the acceptance a novice must have of their new life. The bottom line is perseverance. One must have that. If the new hopeful is looking for the perfect monastery—it does not exist. It does exist, however, in one's self. The monk must accept the drawbacks, quirks, etc. of the others within the community. Not dwell on these aspects of life but go forward and live according to his outlook and concept of life. Perseverance is the key one must have to live in community. One thing is certain, as a monk told me, "Nightly recreation can be tough after the first two weeks. It's not all that one might imagine. It's the same people every night, year in and year out. Think about it."

Each of the twenty-two monks who live at the monastery is on a personal journey. They come from different corners of the world: America, Mexico, Philippines, England, Vietnam, Argentina, and Taiwan. All are solitary, reverent men who feel something missing in their lives.

Community continually comes up, the community of the monastery just as community in life. Whether it's the world, the city, the neighborhood, or the family. Sometimes things are so simple, but within me there is always questioning and doubts. Philip told me, "In a monastery like this, you have to grow or you have to leave, because we don't have any outlets. A contemplative community simply focuses on the interior life, period. One must take a real personal approach. It's like a marriage or any relationship."

Using crumbs of bread with sugar and tea, matchsticks, a pop-top from a soda can, a piece of wire from a broom tool, and cigarette ash we secretly crafted prayer beads. It was our own little factory, our own little community. We saved them as gifts for our loved ones and for the guards who fed us. Our factory was not shut down. On the day of my release Nadr Ali was allowed to accompany me to the stairs of our cellblock to say our final good-bye. Throughout our time together he was more concerned for my freedom and my well-being than for his own: "You are going to be free, Tony. Tell your mother '*salaam alaikum*' from me."

Since coming home to New Mexico after my release I hadn't had time to sort everything out. The two situations were similar in a bizarre way—being in prison is like monastic life. Both were times of reflection.

I spoke with one of the monks about the offices and reading the Psalms. He gave me a wonderful insight. For the monks singing the Psalms (the offices) is work. It is the Work of God. It helped put much into perspective for me. It is so simple. There is work, the everyday manual labors of the monastery, and there is the everyday Work of God. There is also the daily inner conflict—it is a constant. I realized that my photography is a form of prayer for me. There is no need to chase it, patience; it will always come, just as the light.

Last night Philip discussed his role as prior with the monks at chapter. That also was quite enlightening. He did it using *The Rule* of Benedict as a framework. In asking for input from the monks it was only the older monks who spoke up. Christopher brought up the question of the prior as a mediator, Bernie the question of access to the prior and the role of computers in monastic life, Leander the question of fairness, and Gerald the idea that all the monks are priors and the prior a monk. Fairness, objectivity, and caring were all part of the discussion.

There are times along the way when I have realized what an incredible opportunity and gift I have been given to be able to join the community and live as a monk. I have said to myself: "Embrace this life you have been given." Yes it will end, but while I am part of it, living within the monastic community, embrace it. When it ends, I will never be able to reenter this world. I will be a guest again, not a member. That I will mourn, but while I am able, learn from it, feel it, and live it. And as I sit here writing, I see that it is life that I am talking about. It is so simple, but I have never understood it in this context. Don't erect barriers. Stay open and move forward.

Yesterday evening at vespers, calmness returned. What happens with the story I cannot fret or worry about. It is what happens within me that is the essence of my being here. What I can learn about myself and take with me into the next chapter of my life. Accept all the blessings that have been given to me. The struggle is far from over, but once again just carry on. Have faith in life. Mr. Sámi, my interrogator in prison, had told me I had to surrender the gold medallion I wore, a keepsake from Dad that I had kept after his death. I refused, believing I would never see it again, finally acquiescing only after his oath that he would return it to me on my release. As I walked through the prison door, stepping into the sunlight of the prison yard I sensed an old man staring at me as I passed into freedom. His hand extended, he dropped the gold medallion of Mother and Child into my open hand. "Mr. Sámi" were his only words.

I am not a monk, I am an observer. These men who give their lives to God, they are the monks, the bearers of a ritual that for centuries has provided a safe haven for those on their own spiritual journey.

They allowed me into their lives, their way of life. For me it's been a period of learning to slow down, of keeping it simple, of letting the photograph come to me, of waiting in silence, waiting for the light.

The Monastery of Christ in the Desert,
January–December 1995

To My Parents, Bill and Inez, with Love

Acknowledgments

WHERE DOES ONE BEGIN? There have been so many people who have touched my life and encouraged me along my way. To name them all would be impossible. I can only say I hope through this book I can express my humble thanks.

However, I would like to take this opportunity to thank John Scanlon, a dear friend and mentor, and the Scanlon Family Foundation for making the publication of this book possible.

Thank you to my family, Kiera, Brenna, Liam, and Petra, my friend and editor, for your unending love and support, and to Nadr Ali, my spiritual brother. Thank you to the good brothers of the Monastery of Christ in the Desert, especially Abbot Philip. I would also like to thank Mother Rose and the dear sisters of Mt. Carmel.

Christopher Merrill, thank you for your trust and beautiful words. Thank you to Mary Wachs, editorial director at Museum of New Mexico Press, and David Skolkin, art director, for your patience and belief in my work.

Thank you Mary Anne Redding, Daniel Kosharek, Alyssa Marquis (F22), Claudia Dowling, Chris Franke, Brian Healey, Joanna Hurley, Steve Dunn, Brian Moe, and Walter Nelson. Thank you Friedl and Martha.

Project editor: Mary Wachs
Design and production: David Skolkin
Composition: Set in Requiem
Manufactured in Malaysia
10 9 8 7 6 5 4 3 2 1

Library of Congress Cataloging-in-Publication Data
O'Brien, Tony, 1946-
  Light in the desert : photographs from the Monastery of Christ in the Desert / photographs by Tony O'Brien ; with an essay by Christopher Merrill ; foreword by Mary Anne Redding. —1st.
    p. cm.
  ISBN 978-0-89013-533-4 (clothbound : alk. paper) 1. Monastery of Christ in the Desert (Abiquiu, N.M.)—Pictorial works. I. Merrill, Christopher. II. Title.
  BX2525.M66O27 2011
  246'.9708828278952--dc22
                              2011010119

Museum of New Mexico Press
Post Office Box 2087
Santa Fe, New Mexico 87504
www.mnmpress.org